WRITING WITH EASE, REVISED EDITION

Level One

part of *The Complete Writer*

STUDENT PAGES

By

Susan Wise Bauer

Peter Buffington

Susanna Jarrett

WELL-TRAINED MIND PRESS

18021 The Glebe Lane
Charles City, VA 23030
www.welltrainedmind.com

Names:
Bauer, Susan Wise, author. | Buffington, Peter, author. | Jarrett, Susanna, author.
Title:
Writing with ease. Level one, Student pages / by Susan Wise Bauer, Peter Buffington, Susanna Jarrett.
Description:
Revised edition. | Charles City, VA : Well-Trained Mind Press, [2023] | Series: The complete writer | Interest age level: 005-007.
Identifiers:
ISBN: 978-1-945841-55-2 (paperback)
Subjects:
LCSH: English language--Rhetoric--Study and teaching (Elementary) | English language-- Composition and exercises--Study and teaching (Elementary) | LCGFT: Problems and exercises. | BISAC: JUVENILE NONFICTION / Language Arts / Composition & Creative Writing.
Classification:
LCC: LB1576 .B38 2023 | DDC: 372.62/3--dc23

1 2 3 4 5 6 7 8 9 10 B&B 31 30 29 28 27 26 25 24 23

Cover Design by Shane Klink

Date ______________________

Name ____

Week 1
Day One

Copywork

There were no roads.

The deer and the rabbits would be shy and swift.

Date ____________________

Name ____________________

Narration

From *Little House in the Big Woods,* by Laura Ingalls Wilder

What is one thing you remember about the passage?

Date ______________________

Week 1
Day Three

Name ____

Copywork

Pa owned a pig.

There was plenty of fresh meat to last for a long time.

Date ______________________

Name ____

Week 1
Day Four

Narration

From *Little House in the Big Woods*, by Laura Ingalls Wilder

What is one thing you remember about the passage?

Date ______________________

Name ______________________

Week 1
Day Five

Creative Writing

Instructor

Student

Date ______________________

Name ______________________

Week 2
Day One

Copywork

Geppetto made Pinocchio.

Geppetto decided to make a wooden puppet named Pinocchio.

Date ______________________

Name ______________________

Narration

From *The Adventures of Pinocchio,* by Carlo Collodi

What is one thing you remember about the passage?

Date ______________________

Name ____

Week 2
Day Three

Copywork

The puppet was Pinocchio.

Geppetto made the puppet Pinocchio out of wood.

Date ____________________

Name ____

Narration

From *The Adventures of Pinocchio,* by Carlo Collodi

What is one thing you remember about the passage?

Date ____________________

Name ____

Creative Writing

Instructor

Student

Date ____________________

Name ____________________

Week 3
Day One

Copywork

A poor miller had a daughter.

Once upon a time a poor miller had a beautiful daughter.

Date ______________________

Name ____

Narration

From *The Blue Fairy Book,* by Andrew Lang

What is one thing you remember about the passage?

Date ____________________

Name ______________________________________

Week 3
Day Three

Copywork

His name was Rumpelstiltzkin.

She asked him if his name was Sheepshanks or Cruickshanks.

Date ____________________

Name ____________________

Narration

From *The Blue Fairy Book,* by Andrew Lang

What is one thing you remember about the passage?

Date ____________________

Name ____

Creative Writing

The cow ________ for hours.

The pig ________ to the tune of Happy Birthday.

The dog ________ all the way home.

danced burped skipped

Date ______________________

Week 4
Day One

Name ____

Copywork

Alice was silent.

The caterpillar was the first to speak.

Date ______________________

Name ____

Narration

From *Alice's Adventures in Wonderland*, by Lewis Carroll

What is one thing you remember about the passage?

Date ____________________

Name ____________________

Week 4
Day Three

Copywork

The first witness was the Hatter.

One of the jurors had a pencil that squeaked.

Date ____________________

Name ____________________

Narration and Copywork

From *Alice's Adventures in Wonderland,* by Lewis Carroll

What is one thing you remember about the passage?

Instructor

Student

Name ______________________ Date ______________________

Creative Writing

Instructor

Student

Date ______________________

Name ______________________________________

Copywork

Jacob Grimm wrote down fairy tales.

Jacob Grimm and Wilhelm Grimm were brothers who collected fairy tales.

Date ______________________

Name ____

Narration

From "The Frog Prince," by Jacob and Wilhelm Grimm

What is one thing you remember about the passage?

Date

Week 5
Day Three

Name

Copywork

Edgar Taylor translated the fairy tales.

Edgar Taylor and Marian Edwardes translated the fairy tales into English.

Date ____________________

Name ____________________

Narration and Copywork

From "The Frog Prince," by Jacob and Wilhelm Grimm

What is one thing you remember about the passage?

Instructor

Student

Date ______________________

Name ______________________

Creative Writing

Instructor

Student

Name ____________________ Date ____________________

Copywork

Jane and Michael Banks stared.

Jane and Michael Banks stared at their new nanny, Mary Poppins.

Date ____________________

Name ____________________

Narration

From *Mary Poppins*, by P. L. Travers

What is one thing you remember about the passage?

Copywork

Mary Poppins gave Jane and Michael medicine.

Mary Poppins taught Jane and Michael Banks how to say the word supercalifragilisticexpialidocious.

Date ______________________

Name ____

Narration and Copywork

From *Mary Poppins,* by P. L. Travers

What is one thing you remember about the passage?

Instructor

Student

Date ____________________

Name ____

Creative Writing

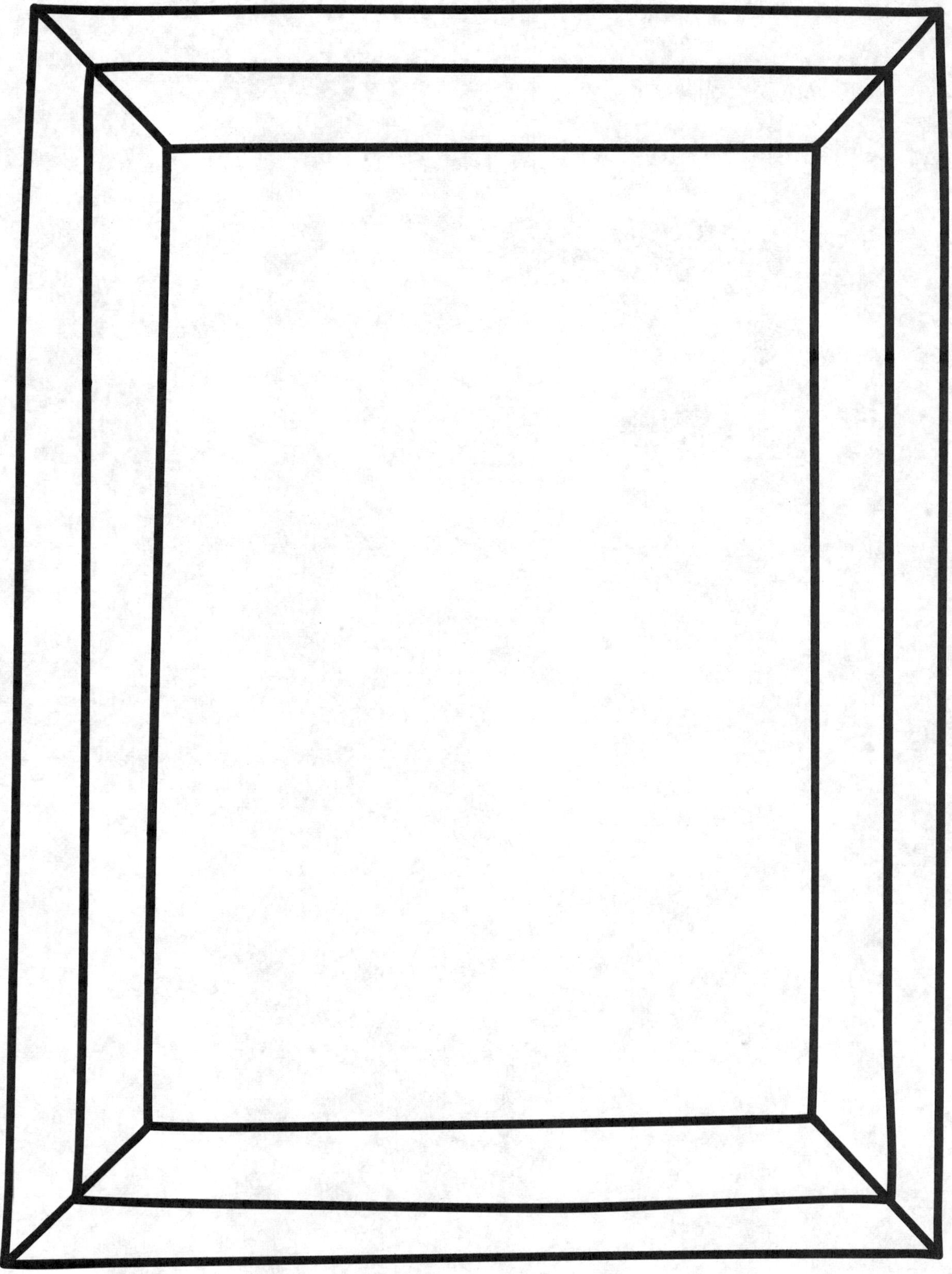

Date ______________________

Name ____

Week 7
Day One

Copywork

Peter Rabbit lived under a fir tree.

Flopsy, Mopsy, and Cottontail were good little bunnies.

Date ______________________

Name ______________________

Narration

From *The Tale of Peter Rabbit,* by Beatrix Potter

What is one thing you remember about the passage?

Date ____________________

Name ____________________

Week 7
Day Three

Copywork

Beatrix Potter was born in London.

Beatrix Potter was born in London, but she bought a farm in Sawrey, England.

Date ______________________

Name ____

Narration and Copywork

From *The Tale of Peter Rabbit,* by Beatrix Potter

What is one thing you remember about the passage?

Instructor

Student

Date ______________________

Name ______________________

Creative Writing

Instructor

Student

Copywork

The Woodlawn family was from Boston.

Caddie Woodlawn and her family moved to the state of Wisconsin.

Date ______________________

Name ____

Narration

From *Caddie Woodlawn,* by Carol Ryrie Brink

What is one thing you remember about the passage?

Date ____________________

Name ____

Copywork

The circuit rider was from Boston.

The circuit rider rode all over the state of Wisconsin.

Date ______________________

Name ______________________

Narration and Copywork

From *Caddie Woodlawn,* by Carol Ryrie Brink

What is one thing you remember about the passage?

Instructor

Student

Date ______________________

Name ______________________

Creative Writing

Instructor

Student

Date ______________________

Name ______________________

Copywork

The school bus honked from the road.

The teacher asked Fern to name the capital of Pennsylvania.

Date ______________________

Name ____

Narration

From *Charlotte's Web,* by E. B. White

What is one thing you remember about the passage?

Date ____________________

Name ____________________

Copywork

She named him Wilbur.

Fern took no notice of the others on the bus.

Narration and Copywork

From *Charlotte's Web,* by E. B. White

What is one thing you remember about the passage?

Instructor

Student

Date ______________________

Name ____

Creative Writing

Date ____________________

Name ____

Copywork

Davy Crockett was born in Tennessee.

Davy Crockett lived in Tennessee, but he wanted to explore Texas.

Date ______________________

Name ______________________

Narration

From *Davy Crockett, Young Rifleman,* by Aileen Wells Parks

What is one thing you remember about the passage?

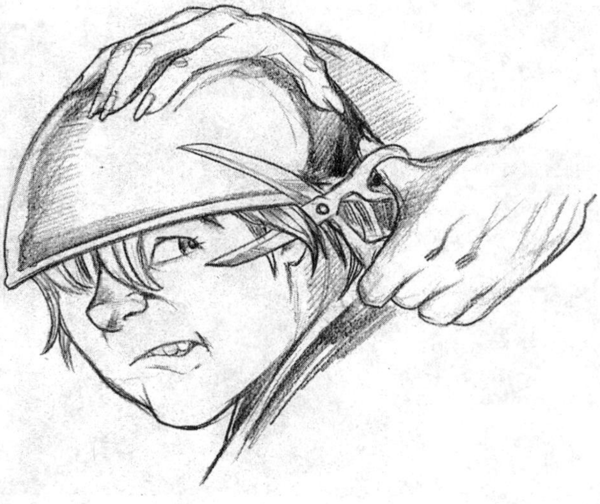

Date ______________________

Name ____

Copywork

Sacagawea belonged to the Shoshoni tribe.

Sacagawea helped Meriwether Lewis and William Clark explore the Missouri River.

Date ______________________

Name ____

Narration and Copywork

From *Sacagawea: American Pathfinder,* by Flora Warren Seymour

What is one thing you remember about the passage?

Instructor

Student

Date ______________________

Name ______________________

Creative Writing

Instructor

Student

Date ________________________

Name ____

Week 11
Day One

Copywork

Louis is a musician.

He came here from Montana with Sam Beaver.

Date ______________________________

Name ______________________________

Narration

From *The Trumpet of the Swan,* by E. B. White

What is one thing you remember about the passage?

Date ______________________

Name ______________________________________

Copywork

Louis had no trouble finding Philadelphia.

They flew south across Maryland and Virginia.

Date ______________________

Name ______________________

Narration and Copywork

From *The Trumpet of the Swan,* by E. B. White

What is one thing you remember about the passage?

Instructor

Student

Date ______________________

Name ____

Creative Writing

Instructor

Student

Name ______________________ Date ______________________

Week 12
Day One

Copywork

Today is Monday, today is Monday.

Today is Wednesday, today is Wednesday. Wednesday is soup day.

Date ____________________

Name ____________________

Narration

From "Today Is Monday"

What is one thing you remember about the passage?

Date ____________________

Name ____________________

Week 12
Day Three

Copywork

On Thursday we eat roast beef.

Today is Friday. On Friday we clean the house from top to bottom.

Date ____________________

Name ____________________

Narration and Copywork

From "Old Mother Hubbard," by Anonymous

What is one thing you remember about the passage?

Instructor

Student

Date ______________________

Name ______________________________________

Creative Writing

On ______________ I will ______________
______________________________________.

On ______________ I will ______________
______________________________________.

On ______________ I will ______________
______________________________________.

Date ______________________

Name ____

Copywork

Rain is for Saturday and Sunday.

Good weather is for Monday, Tuesday, Wednesday, Thursday, and Friday.

Date ______________________

Name ____

Narration

From *The Saturdays,* by Elizabeth Enright

What is one thing you remember about the passage?

Date ______________________

Name ____

Copywork

Saturday dawned much the same as any other day.

When Randy woke up, she had the same feeling in her stomach that she always had on Christmas Day.

Date ______________________

Name ____

Narration and Copywork

From *The Saturdays,* by Elizabeth Enright

What is one thing you remember about the passage?

Instructor

Student

Date ______________________

Name ____

Creative Writing

Instructor

Student

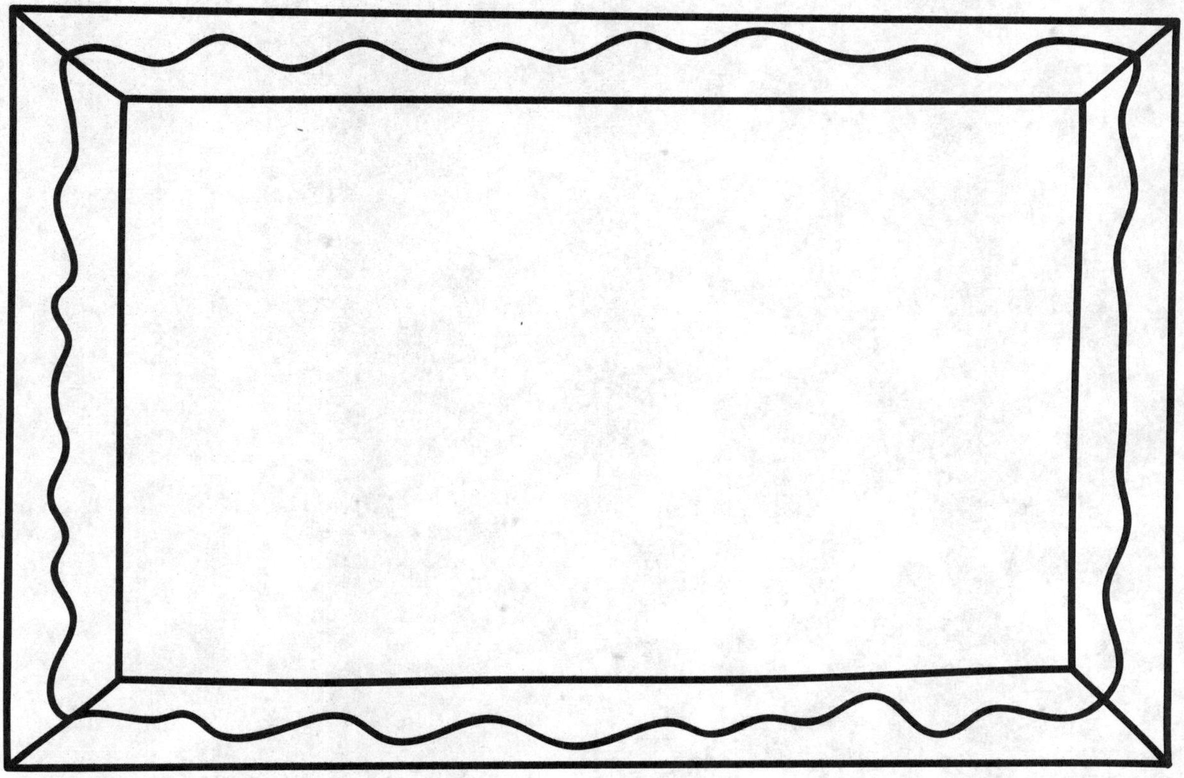

Date ______________________

Week 14
Day One

Name ______________________________________

Copywork

Thirty days hath September,
April, June, and November.
All the rest have thirty-one,
Except for February alone.
Which has four and twenty-four,
Til leap year gives it one day more.

The month of December has 31 days.

The months of January, March, August, and October all have 31 days.

Date ______________________

Name ____

Narration

From "Bed in Summer," by Robert Louis Stevenson

Why is the child unhappy?

Date ______________________

Name ____

Copywork

June and July are summer months.

December and January are winter months, but March is a spring month.

Date ________________________

Name ____

Narration and Copywork

Traditional folk tale, adapted by Susan Wise Bauer

What is one thing you remember about the passage?

Instructor

Student

Date

Name

Week 14
Day Five

Creative Writing

Instructor

Student

Date ______________

Name ______________

Week 15
Day One

Copywork

But in June came three wet days.

It was September, and the turf was dry and crisp.

Date ____________________

Name ____________________

Narration

From *The Railway Children,* by Edith Nesbit

What is one thing you remember about the passage?

Date ____________________

Name ____________________

Copywork

But it happened to be a wet day and, for July, very cold.

They had seen the blossom on the trees in the spring, and they knew where to look for wild cherries.

Date ______________________

Name ____

Narration and Copywork

From *The Railway Children,* by Edith Nesbit

What is one thing you remember about the passage?

Instructor

Student

Date ______________________________

Week 15
Day Five

Name ______________________________

Creative Writing

Instructor

Student

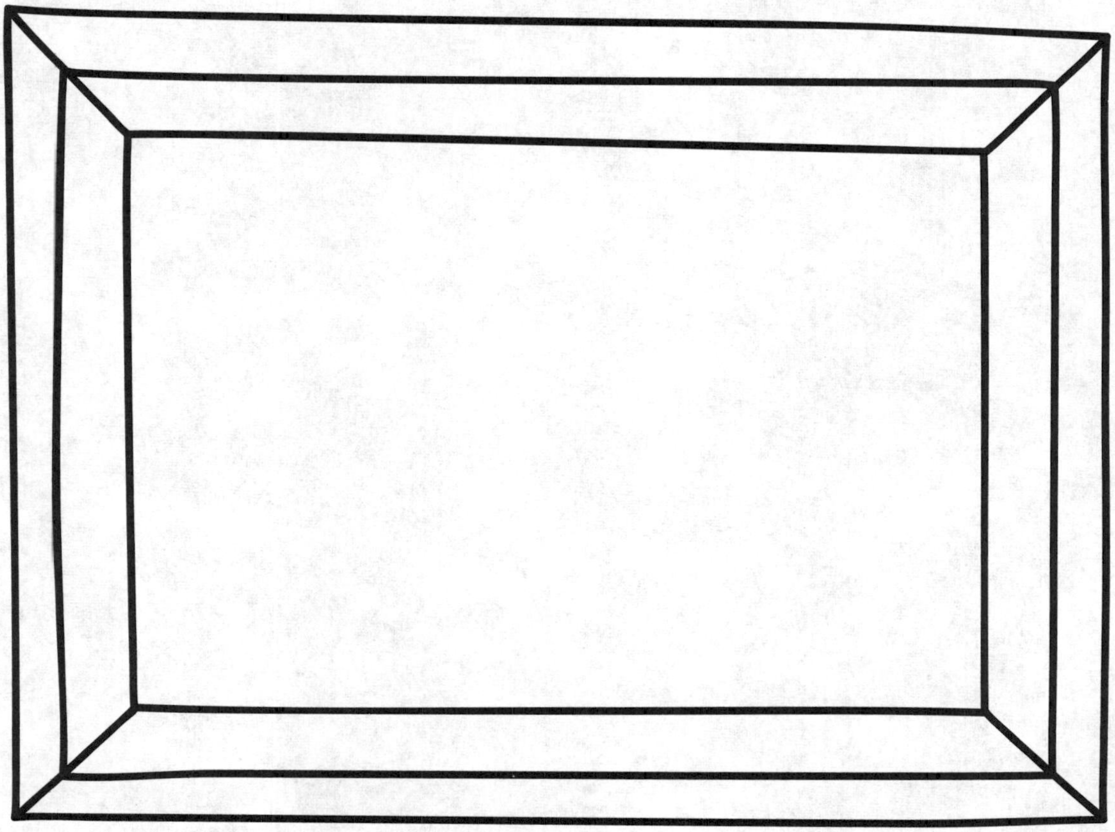

Date ______________________

Week 16
Day One

Name ____

Copywork

Today is ____________________, ______________ ______, __________.
(day of the week) (month) (day) (year)

I was born on ____________________, ____________ ______, __________.
(day of the week) (month) (day) (year)

Date ______________________

Name ____

Narration

From "Master of All Masters," folk tale retold by Joseph Jacobs

What is one thing you remember about the passage?

Date ______________________

Name ____

Copywork

Aesop was a slave who lived in ancient Greece.

Aesop lived on an island called Samos. He once visited Athens, the greatest city in Greece.

Date ____________________

Name ______________________________

Narration and Copywork

From "The Dog and His Reflection," by Aesop

What is one thing you remember about the passage?

Instructor

Student

Date ______________________

Name ____

Creative Writing

The angry buffalo	twirled to the music.
The lonely shark	ate too much candy.
The dancing penguin	ran home.

Date ______________________

Name ____

Week 17
Day One

Copywork

You know about sheep, and I know about dragons.

I always said, you know, that that cave up there was a dragon-cave.

Date ________________________

Name ____

Narration

From *The Reluctant Dragon*, by Kenneth Grahame

What is one thing you remember about the passage?

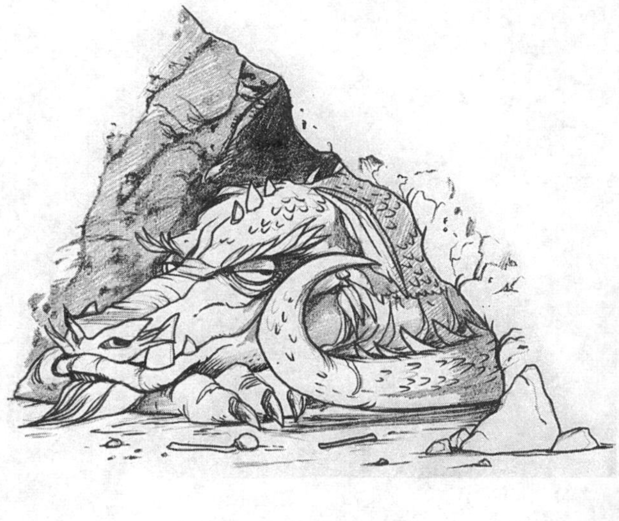

Date ____________________

Name ____________________

Copywork

You must tell him that I will not fight.

In the old days, I always let the other dragons do all the fighting.

Date ____________________

Name ____________________

Narration and Copywork

From *The Reluctant Dragon,* by Kenneth Grahame

What is one thing you remember about the passage?

Instructor

Student

Date ____________________

Name ____________________

Week 17
Day Five

Creative Writing

Instructor

Student

Name ______________________________ Date ______________

Copywork

It was a warm day, and he had a long way to go.

Outside his house he found Piglet, jumping up and down trying to reach the knocker.

Date ____________________

Name ____________________

Week 18
Day Two

Narration

From *Winnie-the-Pooh,* by A. A. Milne

What is one thing you remember about the passage?

Date

Name

Copywork

He dropped his pine cone into the river.

But then he thought he would just look at the river instead, because it was a peaceful sort of day.

Date ____________________

Name ____________________

Narration and Copywork

From *The House at Pooh Corner,* by A. A. Milne

What is one thing you remember about the passage?

Instructor

Student

Date ______________________

Name ____

Creative Writing

Instructor

Student

Date ____________________

Name ____________________

Copywork

When she was angry, her little eyes flashed blue.

The wrinkles of contempt crossed the wrinkles of peevishness, and made her face as full of wrinkles as a pat of butter.

Date ____________________

Name ____

Narration

From *The Light Princess*, by George MacDonald

What is one thing you remember about the passage?

Date ______________________

Name ____

Copywork

They soon found out that the princess was missing.

The wind carried her off through the opposite window and away.

Date ____________________

Name ____

Narration and Copywork

From *The Light Princess*, by George MacDonald

What is one thing you remember about the passage?

Instructor

Student

Date ____________________

Name ____________________

Creative Writing

Date ______________________________ Week 20
Day One

Name ____

Copywork

A. A. Milne wrote stories about Piglet and Pooh.

The writer A. A. Milne really did have a son named Christopher Robin.

Date

Week 20
Day Two

Name

Narration

From *A Child's Geography of the World,* by V. M. Hillyer

What is one thing you remember about the passage?

Date ______________________

Name ____

Copywork

V. M. Hillyer wrote a book about geography for children.

V. M. Hillyer thought that children should also study maps, collect stamps, and make scrapbooks about the world.

Date ______________________

Name ____

Week 20
Day Four

Narration and Copywork

From *A Child's Geography of the World,* by V. M. Hillyer

What is one thing you remember about the passage?

Instructor

Student

Date ______________________

Name ____

Creative Writing

Instructor

Student

Date ________________________

Name ____

Week 21
Day One

Copywork

My full name is ________________ ________________ ________________.
(first name) (middle name) (last name)

My initials are __________ __________ __________.
(first initial) (middle initial) (last initial)

My parent's full name is ________________ ________________ ________________.
(first name) (middle name) (last name)

My parent's initials are __________ __________ __________.
(first initial) (middle initial) (last initial)

Date

Name

Narration

From *The Adventures of Tom Sawyer,* by Mark Twain

What is one thing you remember about the passage?

Date ______________________

Name ______________________

Copywork

Jim came skipping out at the gate with a tin pail.

Saturday morning was come, and all the summer world was bright and fresh, and brimming with life.

Date ______________________

Name ____

Narration and Copywork

From *The Adventures of Tom Sawyer,* by Mark Twain

What is one thing you remember about the passage?

Instructor

Student

Date ______________________

Name ____

Creative Writing

Instructor

Student

Date ____________________

Name ____________________

Week 22
Day One

Copywork

They played in the garden in spring.

In spring, the boy and the rabbit spent long days in the garden.

Name ______________________ Date ______________

Narration

From *The Velveteen Rabbit*, by Margery Williams Bianco

What is one thing you remember about the passage?

Date

Name

Week 22
Day Three

Copywork

That was a wonderful summer.

In the spring, the boy went out to play in the wood.

Date ____________________

Name ____________________

Narration and Copywork

From *The Velveteen Rabbit*, by Margery Williams Bianco

What is one thing you remember about the passage?

Instructor

Student

Date

Week 22
Day Five

Name

Creative Writing

Instructor

Student

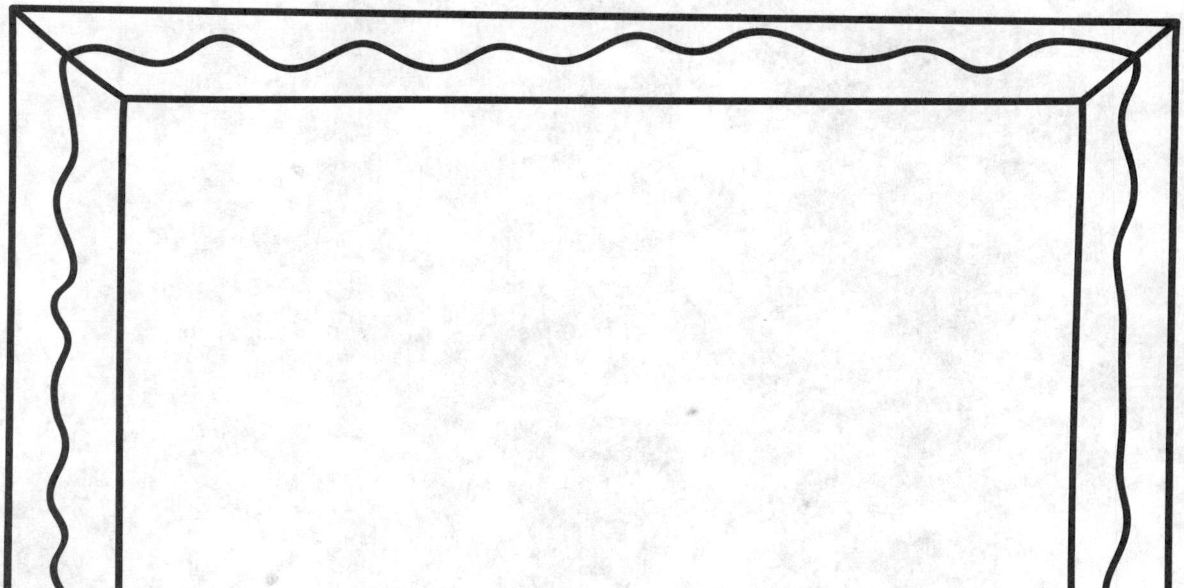

Date ______________________

Name ____

Copywork

Billy dangled a leaf in front of the cat.

Joe came scuffing up the walk and flopped down beside Billy.

Date ____________________

Name ____

Narration

From *How to Eat Fried Worms,* by Thomas Rockwell

What is one thing you remember about the passage?

Date ______________________

Name ____

Copywork

And I will not eat them all at once.

Last week I put in the five dollars my grandmother gave me.

Date ______________________

Name ______________________

Week 23
Day Four

Narration and Copywork

From *How to Eat Fried Worms*, by Thomas Rockwell

What is one thing you remember about the passage?

Instructor

Student

Date ______________________

Name ____

Creative Writing

Instructor

Student

Date ______________________

Name ______________________

Week 24
Day One

Copywork

January . . . .

February . . . . . .

March . . . .

April . . . .

May (we do not abbreviate May)

June . . . .

July . . . .

August . . . .

September . . . . .

October . . . .

November. . . . . .

December. . . . . .

Date ______________________

Name ____

Narration

From *The Happy Hollisters,* by Jerry West

What is one thing you remember about the passage?

Date ____________________

Name ____

Week 24
Day Three

Copywork

Today is ____________________, ____________________ ______, __________.
(day of the week) (month) (day) (year)

Today is ____________________, ______________ ______, __________.
(day of the week) (month abbrev.) (day) (year)

I was born on ____________________ ______, __________.
(month) (day) (year)

I was born on ______________ ______, __________.
(month abbrev.) (day) (year)

Date ____________________

Name ______________________________________

Narration and Copywork

From *The Happy Hollisters*, by Jerry West

What is one thing you remember about the passage?

Instructor

Student

Date ____________________

Name ____

Creative Writing

Instructor

Student

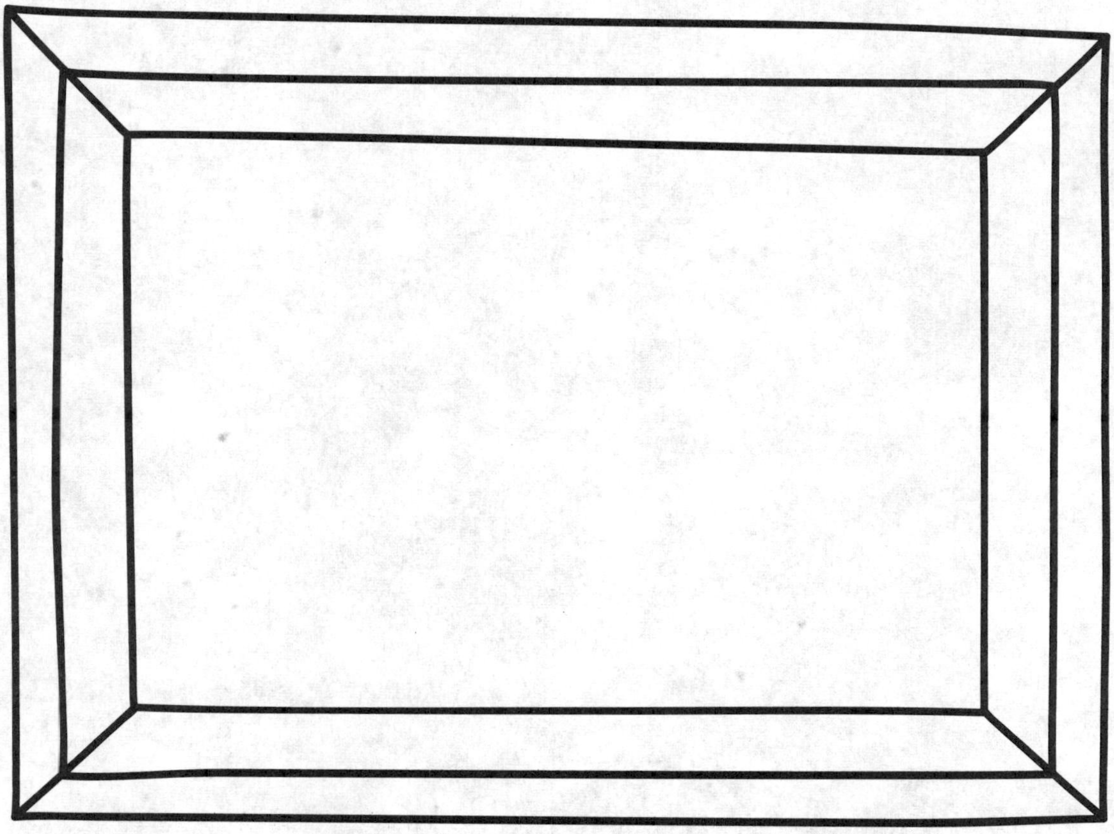

Date ______________________

Name ______________________________________

Week 25
Day One

Copywork

Now sit down, please, right here.

She used to come and sit on our doorstep with the kids.

Date ______________________

Name ______________________

Narration

From *Pollyanna*, by Eleanor Porter

What is one thing you remember about the passage?

Date ______________________

Name ____

Week 25
Day Three

Copywork

She set the pitcher down at once.

Pollyanna was disappointed, and she set the bowl of jelly down.

Date ____________________

Name ____________________

Narration and Copywork

From *Pollyanna,* by Eleanor Porter

What is one thing you remember about the passage?

Instructor

Student

Name ______________________ Date ______________

Creative Writing

Instructor

Student

Date ______________________

Name ____

Copywork

From here they looked down into the garden of Mr. McGregor.

The gig was driven by Mr. McGregor, and beside him sat Mrs. McGregor in her best bonnet.

Date ______________________

Name ____

Narration

From *The Tale of Benjamin Bunny*, by Beatrix Potter

What is one thing you remember about the passage?

Date

Name

Week 26
Day Three

Copywork

Old Mrs. Rabbit was a widow.

The name of the father of Benjamin was Mr. Benjamin Bunny.

Date ______________________

Name ____

Narration and Copywork

From *The Tale of Benjamin Bunny*, by Beatrix Potter

What is one thing you remember about the passage?

Instructor

Student

Date ______________________________

Name ____

Creative Writing

Instructor

Student

Date ____________

Name ____________

Week 27
Day One

Copywork

In came Mrs. Fezziwig, one vast substantial smile.

I have the pleasure of addressing Mr. Scrooge and Mr. Marley.

Date ____________________

Name ____________________

Narration

From *A Christmas Carol*, by Charles Dickens

What is one thing you remember about the passage?

Date ____________________

Name ____

Copywork

Mr. Scrooge it was.

In came the three Miss Fezziwigs, beaming and lovable.

Date

Name

Week 27
Day Four

Narration and Copywork

From *A Christmas Carol*, by Charles Dickens

What is one thing you remember about the passage?

Instructor

Student

Date ____________________

Name ______________________________

Creative Writing

Instructor

Student

Date

Name

Week 28
Day One

Copywork

In the morning Mr. Scott slid down the rope and dug.

The buckets came up full of mud, and Pa and Mr. Scott worked every day in deeper mud.

Date ____________________

Name ____

Narration

From *Little House on the Prairie,* by Laura Ingalls Wilder

What is one thing you remember about the passage?

Date ______________________

Name ____

Copywork

Grasshoppers beat down from the sky and swarmed thick over the ground.

Millions and millions of grasshoppers were eating now. You could hear the millions of jaws biting and chewing.

Name

Date

Narration and Copywork

From *On the Banks of Plum Creek,* by Laura Ingalls Wilder

What is one thing you remember about the passage?

Instructor

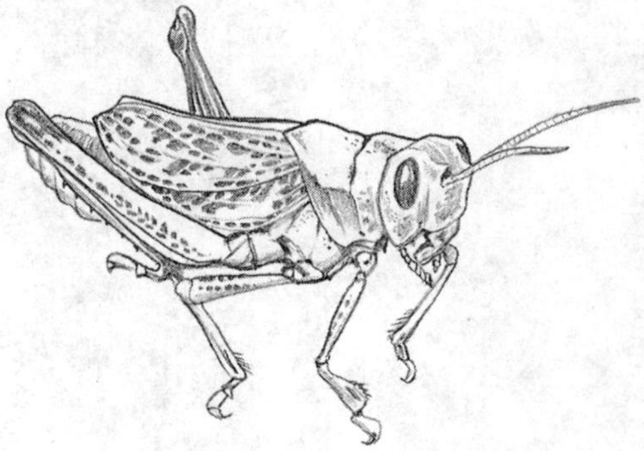

Student

Date ____________________

Name ______________________________________

Creative Writing

Instructor

Student

Date ____________________

Name ____________________

Week 29
Day One

Copywork

I am Miss Allen, your new librarian.

You know how Tillie never takes a book out herself, but she is always wanting to read mine.

Date

Name

Week 29
Day Two

Narration

From *All-of-a-Kind Family,* by Sydney Taylor

What is one thing you remember about the passage?

Date ____________________

Name ____________________

Copywork

Sarah studied the new library lady anxiously.

She has dimples, Sarah thought. Surely a lady with dimples could never be harsh.

Date ______________________

Name ____

Narration and Copywork

From *All-of-a-Kind Family*, by Sydney Taylor

What is one thing you remember about the passage?

Instructor

Student

Date ______________________

Name ____

Creative Writing

Instructor

Student

Date ______________________

Name ____

Copywork

Splash, splash, splash, went her tears again.

Once upon a time there was a deep and wide river, and in this river lived a crocodile.

Date ______________________

Name ______________________

Week 30
Day Two

Narration

From *The Giant Crab and Other Tales from Old India*, retold by W. H. D. Rouse

What is one thing you remember about the passage?

Date ______________________

Name ______________________

Copywork

W. H. D. Rouse wrote new versions of many Jataka Tales.

W. H. D. Rouse, along with T. E. Page, edited a series of famous books about classic works of literature.

Date ______________________

Name ____

Narration and Copywork

From *The Giant Crab and Other Tales from Old India,* retold by W. H. D. Rouse.

What is one thing you remember about the passage?

Instructor

Student

Date ______________________

Name ______________________

Creative Writing

Instructor

Student

Date ______________________

Name ____

Week 31
Day One

Copywork

Across the lonely beach we flit,
One little sandpiper and I,
And fast I gather, bit by bit,
The scattered driftwood, bleached and dry.

Date ____________________

Name ____

Narration

From "The Sandpiper," by Celia Thaxter

What is one thing you remember about the passage?

Name ____

Copywork

A nightingale, that all day long
Had cheered the village with his song,
Nor yet at eve his note suspended,
Nor yet when eventide was ended,
Began to feel, as well he might,
The keen demands of appetite.

Date ______________________

Name ____

Narration and Copywork

From "The Nightingale and the Glow-worm," by William Cowper

What is one thing you remember about the passage?

Instructor

Student

Date ____________________

Name ____________________

Creative Writing

Instructor

Student

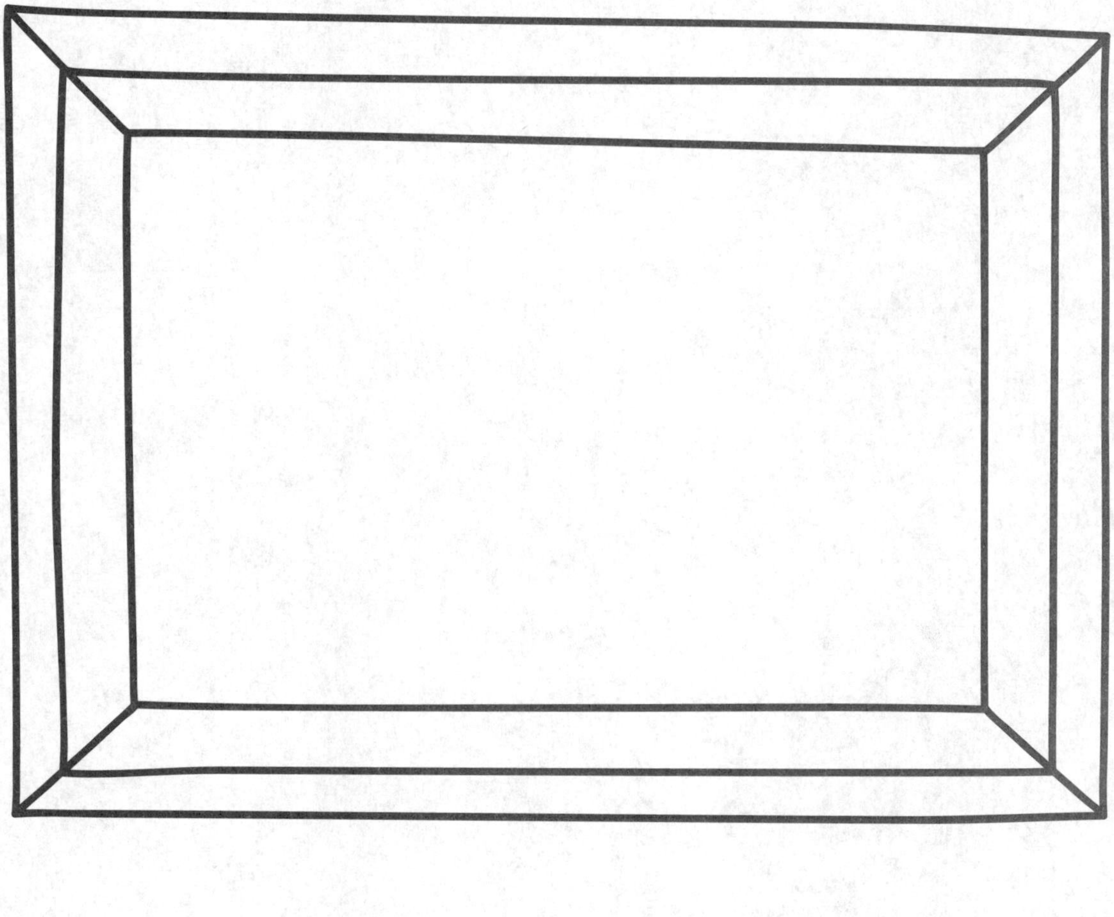

Date ____________________

Name ____________________

Copywork

Come now and deal the stroke.

Take now the axe and let us see how well you can smite.

Date ______________________

Name ____

Narration

From *King Arthur and His Knights of the Round Table,* by Roger Lancelyn Green

What is one thing you remember about the passage?

Date ____________________

Week 32
Day Three

Name ____________________

Copywork

Noble uncle, let this adventure be mine.

See to it that you keep your oath and seek me out a year hence.

Name ______________________________ Date ______________

Narration and Copywork

From *King Arthur and His Knights of the Round Table,* by Roger Lancelyn Green

What is one thing you remember about the passage?

Instructor

Student

Date ______________________

Week 32
Day Five

Name ______________________________________

Creative Writing

Date ______________________

Name ____

Week 33
Day One

Copywork

Have I ever told you about Willy Wonka?

Is it true that his chocolate factory is the biggest in the world?

Date ____________________

Name ____________________

Narration

From *Charlie and the Chocolate Factory,* by Roald Dahl

What is one thing you remember about the passage?

Date ______________________ Week 33

Name ______________________ Day Three

Copywork

Did Mr. Wonka do it?

Have you ever seen a single person going into that place or coming out?

Date ______________________

Name ______________________

Narration and Copywork

From *Charlie and the Chocolate Factory,* by Roald Dahl

What is one thing you remember about the passage?

Instructor

Student

Date

Name

Creative Writing

Instructor

Student

Date

Name

Week 34
Day One

Copywork

I like you!

You are prettier than anything else in the world!

Date ______________________

Name ____

Narration

From *The Secret Garden,* by Frances Hodgson Burnett

What is one thing you remember about the passage?

Date ____________________

Name ____

Copywork

Then I shall see him!

Imagine visiting a cottage that holds twelve children!

Date ______________________

Name ____

Narration and Copywork

From *The Secret Garden,* by Frances Hodgson Burnett

What is one thing you remember about the passage?

Instructor

Student

Date ______________________

Week 34
Day Five

Name ____

Creative Writing

Instructor

Student

Date ____________________

Name ______________________________

Copywork

Is the river so nice as all that?

If you have nothing else on hand this morning, supposing we drop down the river together, and have a long day of it?

Date ____________________

Name ____________________

Narration

From *The Wind in the Willows*, by Kenneth Grahame

What is one thing you remember about the passage?

Date ____________________

Name ____________________

Copywork

This has been a wonderful day!

How black was his despair when he felt himself sinking again!

Date ______________________

Name ____

Narration and Copywork

From *The Wind in the Willows*, by Kenneth Grahame

What is one thing you remember about the passage?

Instructor

Student

Date ______________________

Week 35
Day Five

Name ____

Creative Writing

Instructor

Student

Name ______________________________ Date ______________

Copywork Evaluation

The rain is raining all around,
It falls on field and tree,
It rains on the umbrellas here,
And on the ships at sea.

From *A Child's Garden of Verses,* by Robert Louis Stevenson

Narration Evaluation

From *The Wonderful Wizard of Oz,* by L. Frank Baum

What is one thing you remember about the passage?

Date ______________________________

Name ____

Copywork Evaluation

L. Frank Baum wrote stories about a little girl who lived in Kansas. Her name was Dorothy, and she went to the land of Oz.

Date ______________________

Name ______________________

Narration Evaluation

From *The Wonderful Wizard of Oz,* by L. Frank Baum

What is one thing you remember about the passage?

Instructor

Student